WEDDING STATIONERY

Invitations,

Enclosures,

Thank Yous

& More

JO PACKHAM

A Sterling/Chapelle Book
Sterling Publishing Co., Inc. New York

Jo Packham
Author

Tina Annette Brady
Designer

Cherie Hanson
Editor

Margaret Shields Marti
Executive Editor

Library of Congress Cataloging-in-Publication Data

Packham, Jo.
    Wedding stationery : perfect invitations, enclosures, thank yous &
more / by Jo packham.
        p. cm.
    "A Sterling/Chapelle book."
    Includes index.
    ISBN 0-8069-8831-2
    1. Wedding stationery.   I. Title.
    BJ2092.P33   1993   93-25090
    395' .4--dc20   CIP

10 9 8 7 6 5 4 3 2 1

A Sterling/Chapelle Book

Published by Sterling Publishing Company, Inc.
387 Park Avenue South, New York, N.Y. 10016
© 1993 by Chapelle Ltd.
Distributed in Canada by Sterling Publishing
$^c/_o$ Canadian Manda Group, P.O. Box 920, Station U
Toronto, Ontario, Canada M8Z 5P9
Distributed in Great Britain and Europe by Cassell PLC
Villiers House, 41/47 Strand, London WC2N 5JE, England
Distributed in Australia by Capricorn Link Ltd.
P.O. Box 665, Lane Cove, NSW 2066
Manufactured in the United States of America

Sterling ISBN 0-8069-8831-2

Of all the things which wisdom provides to make life entirely happy, much the greatest is the possession of friendship.

Epicurus

Contents

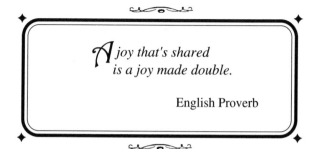

*A joy that's shared
is a joy made double.*

English Proverb

From the first announcement of your
engagement to family and friends to the final
thank-yous sent to all of those who shared in
your special day, the wedding stationery you
select—the type of paper, the kind of engraving,
the style of the writing and the font for the
lettering—is indicative of the style and the
formality of the wedding festivities that
are to be given for and by you.

Tradition has established guidelines for which stationery is appropriate for every style of wedding. Which is the one you will choose? Heavy, white paper and the finest engraving for a very formal wedding? A more informal handwritten, calligraphic note on rose-colored paper for a garden wedding? White paper printed in gold, rolled into a tube that is wrapped with ribbon, and filled with confetti for a contemporary affair?

Whichever you select, you can be creative, within the consistency of style and formality, and make yours the wedding stationery that everyone remembers or uses as an example for their own wedding day.

Basically, there are two categories of stationery to consider:

1. The formal or informal pieces to be used for shower/party invitations, written invitations, printed mementos, and thank-you notes.

2. The formal or informal invitations and enclosures asking guests to the ceremony and/or reception and/or the announcements declaring that the marriage has taken place.

How to Select
a Stationer

If you and the groom have decided on a more traditional, formal wedding or if you simply prefer to have the invitations to some or all of your festivities printed, you will need to find a stationer almost immediately.

As you begin your search for a reliable stationer, the following hints may be helpful:

✦ Ask family and friends for their recommendations.

✦ Ask a local bridal consultant or a wedding coordinator at a large church or synagogue for recommendations.

✦ Look in the Yellow Pages under:

- Stationery stores.
- Wedding shops.
- Department stores that carry wedding attire or stationery products.
- Florists who specialize in weddings.
- Photographers who offer additional wedding services.
- Print shops who cater directly to consumers.
- Other retail stores that deal with all aspects of the wedding trade.

✦ Check mail-order catalogs that offer special stationery products. The names and addresses of these catalogs can be found in bridal magazines. There are advantages and disadvantages to working with this type of stationer. The benefits are:

- The convenience of shopping from your own home.
- Companies are happy to send you a free catalog of samples if you write for them.
- If you are from a small town, they often have a larger selection than you will be able to find locally.

The disadvantages of using a mail-order source are:

- It is often difficult when ordering through a catalog of this nature to find the right person to answer specific questions on specialized items.
- Specialized items are often not available; you are required to order only the products depicted in the catalog.
- It can become more time-consuming to wait for catalogs to be mailed and questions to be answered.

When you select your stationer, follow these suggestions:

✦ Choose two or three stationers from the sources listed on page 9. Make an appointment with each and allow one hour to discuss the details of what you will need to have printed.

✦ Discuss your ideas but keep an open mind. Be flexible and receptive. The stationer may have several ideas to add to your own.

✦ Show samples of stationery items that you have received or collected and pictures you have saved from magazines that depict the look you want.

✦ Give the stationer all of the facts concerning the wedding and the parties that will precede it. The style and formality of the ceremony and reception which include the attire, site, and time of day are important information that the stationer will need.

✦ Look at albums of invitations the stationer has available.

✦ Ask for suggestions and estimates within your budget.

✦ Order all of your invitations, enclosures, and thank-yous at the same time. One large order is much less expensive than several smaller orders. Make certain you know if there is a charge for any specialization you have ordered.

✦ Order one invitation for each married or cohabitating couple that you plan to invite. The officiant and spouse, the attendants, the groomsmen, and all helpers should also receive an invitation. It is not necessary to invite dates of single guests with a separate invitation. If you do elect to send the second party a separate invitation, however, be certain to send it to his or her address and do not write "and Guest" on the inner envelope.

✦ Always order extras of everything. One calculation is approximately 25 percent more than your actual count. This may seem excessive but it is much less expensive to order all at once and have a few extra than to place a very small order because you need just five more! Mistakes will be made, people will be added at the last minute, and you will receive several requests for extras that are going to be kept as mementos.

✦ Request both the outer and inner envelopes to be delivered early so you can address them while the invitations are being printed. This helps if there is less than the desirable amount of time and also aids in alleviating unnecessary time crunches.

✦ Order wedding invitations at least four months prior to the wedding. Plan on three to four weeks for the stationer to fill your order for printed material but make certain you ask him for an exact time from order date to delivery date. Depending on your pre-wedding schedule, allow a minimum of two weeks to address and mail the wedding invitations (longer if you are using a calligrapher). The invitations should be mailed four to six weeks prior to the wedding, or mailed eight weeks prior if your wedding day will be held on a holiday or holiday weekend.

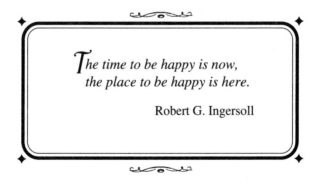

The time to be happy is now,
the place to be happy is here.

Robert G. Ingersoll

Stationer's Checklist

Printer's name _____

Address _____

Phone _____

Items ordered and description: (paper stock, color, type and style of printing)

	Quantity	Cost
❑ Wedding file cards	_____	$ _____

_____

_____

| ❑ Engagement party invitations | _____ | $ _____ |

_____

_____

| ❑ Party/shower invitations | _____ | $ _____ |

_____

_____

| ❑ Rehearsal and rehearsal | _____ | $ _____ |
dinner invitations _____

| ❑ Wedding invitations | _____ | $ _____ |

_____

_____

❑ Delivery date of envelopes _____
   (Outer and Inner)

Enclosure cards:

❑ R.s.v.p. cards _____ $ _____

_____

_____

❑ Ceremony cards _____ $ _____

_____

_____

❑ Ceremony programs _____ $ _____

_____

_____

❑ Reception cards _____ $ _____

_____

_____

❑ Rain cards _____ $ _____

_____

_____

❑ Travel cards _____ $ _____

_____

_____

❑ Maps _____ $ _____

_____

_____

Thank yous:

❑ Showers   _____ $_____

_____

_____

❑ Wedding   _____ $_____

_____

_____

Reception favors:

❑ Napkins   _____ $_____

_____

_____

❑ Matches   _____ $_____

_____

_____

❑ Printed ribbons   _____ $_____

_____

_____

❑ Printed gift boxes   _____ $_____

_____

_____

| | **Total** | $_____ |
| | **Deposit** | $_____ |

Order date _____

Final payment date_____

Delivery date of all

   other printed matter_____

_____

Traditional/Formal

The traditional/formal wedding invitation is white or ivory, with black raised lettering, and contains nothing but the prescribed wording on page 36. The engraving is completed on the top page (the inside is blank) of a double sheet of thick quality paper.

Formal invitations may also contain a family's crest or coat of arms. It is without color and is embossed on the cover of the invitation with the invitation lettering on the inside page. Your family crest or coat of arms is used when your family issues the invitations and announcements. If the groom's family or the groom and you issue the invitations, the groom's coat of arms or crest may be used.

Formal invitations may be addressed by a calligrapher. Enlisting the services of a calligrapher traditionally was very expensive and time-consuming but today many stationery stores have computerized calligraphy machines that create a variety of scripts to choose from.

Contemporary

The contemporary invitation is as individual and memorable as you and the groom wish it to be. Here with the words you use and the presentation you decide upon, you can make an invitation that will be as unique and as remembered as the two of you.

The contemporary invitation may be engraved or printed on colored paper or with colored ink. It may include a poem or a photograph along with the traditional wording. The photograph can be taken of the two of you in a setting in which you associate yourselves. You might want it orchestrated in the woods with autumn leaves falling all around or you could be seated next to one another in a study surrounded by books you both love to read. You might want to consider reproducing black-and-white or brown-sepia-tone photographs of the two of you at a much younger age–anywhere from age two on up. This presentation is guaranteed to bring a smile to the face of each recipient.

Your invitation may be designed to completely break all the rules of tradition by presenting it rolled in a printed tube that is filled with tiny party surprises. It may be tied to the theme of the festivities such as having invitations printed on parchment with burned edges for an Elizabethan-style wedding. These invitations could then be written in Old English by a calligrapher and sealed with a wax seal. You may want to make a Victorian-style invitation with paper lace doilies glued to the top fold of the handmade paper on which it is printed; or, you could fill a brightly colored envelope with heart confetti and have the invitation printed on a coordinating brightly colored paper.

Informal

Informal invitations are often printed on the front of a single heavyweight card. They may be handwritten, purchased preprinted or include any of the combinations in the contemporary section. They need to be selected carefully however, so that they are tasteful and in keeping with the theme and spirit of the wedding ceremony and reception.

The lettering for all styles of invitations are achieved by:

Engraving. This is the most expensive, takes the longest to complete, is the most traditional, and also the most formal. The stationery is pressed onto a copper plate so the letters slightly rise from the page.

Thermography. This is a process that fuses powder and ink to create a raised letter. This takes much less time and is much less expensive because plates do not have to be engraved.

Offset printing. This is the least expensive, the quickest to produce, and offers a variety of styles and colors. It is also the least formal.

Invitations for Parties and Showers

An invitation is any card or note that you send to family and friends for the following two reasons: first, to ask them to join your celebration; and, secondly, to provide them with information—the basic who, what, when, where, and why. Usually, but not always, the invitations sent to invite guests to pre-wedding parties and showers are indicative of the style of wedding you are planning.

The Engagement Party Invitation

If engraved invitations are sent for your engagement party, it is practically a promise that a large formal wedding will follow. If the engagement party is to be less formal, handwritten or purchased invitations are suitable. This is the one occasion in which the invitation may not mention the reason for the party. You may want the announcement of your engagement to be a surprise to your invited guests.

Traditionally, these invitations are sent in the name of your parents but it is becoming more common to have the party hosted and the invitations sent by a relative or friend or maybe even by you and the groom yourselves.

These invitations are sent to guests who include your family and friends, the wedding party, the groom's parents and their family and friends. Whether or not to invite stepfamilies is something you and the groom should consider carefully. Generally, invitations are not sent to guests who will not be invited to the wedding.

The invitations to the engagement party are sent seven to ten days prior to the party, which, traditionally, takes place after you have told immediate family and friends of your engagement and upcoming marriage but before the announcement appears in the newspapers. There is usually six months to one year from the engagement party to the wedding date.

Shower and Party Invitations

No hard-and-fast rules exist regarding the invitations to pre-wedding showers and parties except mailing the invitations two to three weeks prior to each individual occasion. You and the guests are often very busy in the days preceding the ceremony and everyone needs more time than usual to make arrangements.

Invitations to such events are traditionally dictated by the theme of the shower or party. If it is a very formal mother-daughter luncheon or an afternoon tea, then you may want to have the invitations engraved or printed. It is, however, customary to select preprinted invitations, to make your own invitations, or to handwrite invitations that are in keeping with the theme of the festivities.

The Rehearsal

Everyone who is invited to be in the wedding ceremony is invited to the rehearsal although you will want to discourage wedding-party spouses and friends from attending. You will want to send written invitations to those who need to attend the rehearsal, including the time and place. These invitations should be sent three weeks before the wedding.

Rehearsal Dinner Invitation

The invitation to the rehearsal dinner should be in keeping with the style of the wedding invitation and the formality of the event.

Everyone who attends the wedding rehearsal and his/her spouse should be invited to the rehearsal dinner: attendants, clergy, parents and grandparents, parents of children involved in the wedding, out-of-town guests who have arrived, as well as other close friends and relatives. It is up to you and the groom to decide whether or not to include dates and divorced parents (if applicable). If all of the extended families are cordial, it is usually customary to invite both parents and stepparents.

Invitations for the rehearsal dinner should be sent three weeks ahead of time. This guarantees that there will be no questions as to who is invited, when it begins, and how long the evening will last.

An informal rehearsal dinner invitation may be issued on purchased notes with an R.s.v.p. by telephone.

A formal rehearsal dinner invitation may read:

Mr. and Mrs. Anthony Lynn Mathews
request the pleasure of your company
at the Rehearsal Dinner for
Camille Hopkins
and
Terri Mathews
Thursday, the seventeenth day of February
Nineteen hundred and ninety-three
at six o'clock
The Waterfront
1800 Harbor Drive
Newport Beach, California

R.s.v.p.
Mrs. Anthony Mathews
1473 Madison Place
Lake Forest, California 92074

The best portion of a good man's life is his little, nameless unremembered acts of kindness and of love.

William Wordsworth

Thank-You Notes for Shower and Party Hosts and Gifts

Thank-you notes are a very important part of your stationery needs and several points need to be remembered:

+ *All messages on the inside of the thank-yous must be handwritten in all circumstances.*

+ The thank-you notes you select may be whatever you like. They should be appropriate for the specific occasion and/or for the gift that was received.

+ Make certain you purchase a variety of thank-you notes or order a supply of printed or engraved notes beforehand.

+ Only the outside of the note should be printed with a design or with your maiden name printed or engraved. Your maiden name should be on all thank-yous sent before the wedding, your married name on all thank-yous sent after the wedding.

+ Send thank-you notes within one week of attending the shower/party or receiving the shower/party gift.

- Make a list of all parties given and gifts received, being certain each person's name is checked off. Record the reason for the thank-you note and the date that the thank-you note was written and mailed. This list should be a part of your permanent tracking system which is explained on page 31.

- Address the envelope with the giver's name and address before you write the note. Do not forget to write a return address for those thank-you notes that are addressed incorrectly or if the addressee has moved.

- Double-check to make certain that the correct thank-you note is in the correct envelope. Stamp all envelopes at the same time and drop them in the mailbox yourself so you are certain the job is done promptly and correctly.

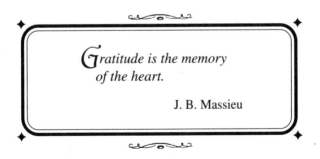

Gratitude is the memory of the heart.

J. B. Massieu

Who is invited to the wedding is a decision that you and the groom will need to agree on as quickly as possible. It is something that needs to be discussed openly so that there are no hard feelings or misunderstandings. The two of you need to agree on a budget and a maximum number of guests (which may be restricted by the site you have selected). That way, if one family is financing the wedding and the other family wishes to invite a larger number of guests, one party does not experience a financial burden it cannot afford.

Once you have decided on how many guests will be included, begin making your list as soon as possible. Because it is so easy to forget someone, it is very important that the list be checked and double-checked. Check your personal phone book, your Christmas card list, any club rosters of which you are a member, your work personnel list, and any family phone books or directories. Carry a pad in your purse to add names as they occur to you.

You may select one of the following options when deciding who invites how many guests:

Option 1: You can divide the list into three even amounts: you and the groom inviting one-third of the guests, your family inviting a third, and the groom's family inviting a third. This seems to be the most fair if one party is paying for the entire wedding.

Option 2: You may decide that you and the groom should invite half of the total number of guests and divide the other half between your two families.

Option 3: If one party wishes to invite a larger number of guests than the other two, it might be decided that they pay the expenses for the extra guests on their list.

When making a list, several circumstances often arise that create questions about whom to invite and whom not to. You may wish to follow the guidelines below or you and your intended may want to discuss each situation separately and make your own decision.

Make certain you check your list against each list given to you by both families. When the final list has been compiled, give both families a copy of the list. This will help familiarize them with whom has been invited and act as a double-check for forgotten or duplicated names.

Special Circumstances

CHILDREN: Children can both add to, and detract from, the events at the wedding. The two of you need to decide if children are to be included in the festivities. Because most caterers charge the full amount for children, inviting them can be expensive and can also fill the allotted number of names on your guest list quite rapidly.

If you choose not to invite children, print either "Adults Only" at the bottom left-hand corner of the invitation or write only the adults' names on the invitation and inner envelopes. If you have a few special children you would like to have attend the wedding and they cannot be included as part of the wedding party, issue a separate invitation addressed only to the children in the family, listing each child's name on the envelope. If some children in one family are over 18 and will be coming with dates and some children are younger and will be accompanying their parents, you will need to send the older children a separate invitation with their names and the words "and Guest" on the inner envelope. The younger children can also receive their own invitation or have their names included on the inner envelope with their parents. It is not advised, however, to invite some children and not others. This could prove awkward for guests who leave their children at home only to see other guests' children at the wedding.

DISTANT RELATIVES/CASUAL FRIENDS: If you are trying to limit the size of your wedding, it is not impolite to invite only close friends and relatives. Distant relatives and friends you seldom see will certainly understand.

PERSONS FROM WHOM YOU HAVE RECEIVED AN INVITATION: If you have been invited to a casual friend's or distant relative's wedding, you should not feel obligated to invite them to yours. This is a very important day in your life and is meant to be shared by those closest to you.

UNINVITED GUESTS: If a friend or relative asks you about the wedding and assumes they will receive an invitation, it should not be embarrassing to explain that the wedding is to be a small one and that you are unable to ask all of those you would like to attend.

In the event that you mistakenly left someone off the list that you really wanted to come, or did not invite someone because you thought they would prefer not to come but they really do, simply call the person, explain the situation, inform them of the details of the wedding festivities, and send them an invitation immediately. Everyone understands that mistakes such as this happen and will surely not think another thing about it.

BUSINESS ASSOCIATES: If your guest list allows room for business associates and fellow employees, then they should be included. After all, you often spend more time with the people at work than you do with family and friends. Remember, however, that you may have to invite a group of people that all associate together at your office in order to avoid hard feelings.

EX-SPOUSES AND EX-IN-LAWS: This is a decision that needs to be made by you, the groom, and all of the families. Traditionally, ex-family members were not invited but it is becoming increasingly acceptable to invite anyone whom you and present family members feel comfortable around.

GUESTS' DATES: Single guests sometimes feel they would enjoy themselves more, and be more comfortable, if they were accompanied by an escort or a date. If the guest does not have a steady partner, write "and Guest" on the inside envelope; if the guest does have a steady partner, and you know the partner, then invite him or her with a separate invitation.

SPECIAL GUESTS: Often situations occur in which you will want to invite special friends or family members even though you are certain they will be unable to attend. In this case, you should send them an invitation to let them know how much you wish they could be with you, sharing in the festivities.

WEDDING PARTICIPANTS: All wedding participants and their spouses, dates or families (of child attendants) should always be invited to both the wedding and the reception.

Address Tracking System

Now is the perfect time to begin a system for keeping all information filed where it is easily obtainable and always current. You will want to develop a system that is easy for you or you may want to use one of the following:

✦ Purchase an address book that has a loose-leaf format so pages can be added as needed.

✦ Start a card file of your own using index cards, alphabetical dividers, and an index box.

Whichever system you select, make certain the following information is gathered from all list maker's and include it on your permanent system:

1. **Names**
   a. Include the husband's, wife's, and children's names in case you need to refer to them at a later time.
   b. You will want to list whose friend or relative each person is so if you are unfamiliar with the name, you will know whom to contact with any questions.

2. **Addresses**
   a. Make certain to include the entire address with city, state and ZIP code.
   b. Write down the date you recorded the address. Since you may use this information for years to come, this will help you determine if the address you have listed is current.

3. Telephone numbers
   a. Include area codes
   b. List home and office numbers of both the husband and the wife.

4. Guest lists

Include a space near the person's name, on the back or on a separate index card to list which events—showers, parties, wedding ceremony and/or reception—he/she was invited to. This will help in several instances. It will act as a safeguard to make certain some friends or relatives do not get invited to too many parties and will act as a double-check to make certain all of those who were invited to showers/parties will receive an invitation to the wedding.

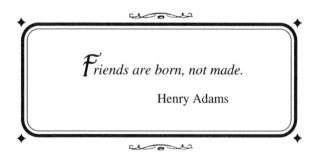

*F*riends are born, not made.

Henry Adams

Wording for the Invitations

Traditionally your parents send the wedding invitations since they host the wedding. When selecting the wording for the invitations, traditional guidelines are as follows:

1. The names at the top of the wedding invitation refer to those persons who are hosting the wedding, not necessarily to those persons who are paying for it.

2. When debating between one wording for an invitation or announcement and another, remember that a name is very special and important to a person.

3. No punctuation is used except after abbreviations, such as "Mr." or "Mrs.," or when phrases requiring separation occur in the same line, as in the date.

4. On formal invitations, all names are spelled out in full without nicknames or the use of initials (Mr. and Mrs. David Samuel Jones). Initials may be used on informal invitations.

5. Spell out numbers, including those in short addresses. If, however, the address is very long, then numerals may be used.

6. Spell out "Junior" if space permits.

7. The date is written, "Saturday, the twenty-sixth of May," with the year spelled out on the following line. It is often accepted to omit the year, if you wish.

8. The time is indicated, "six o'clock" or "half-after six o'clock" (never half past six o'clock).

9. If your ceremony is to be performed in a church and there are churches with similar names in the same city and if many of your guests are from out of town or unfamiliar with the location, the street address should be indicated beneath the name of the ceremony site.

10. "The honour of your presence" is the wording always used for a religious ceremony with "the pleasure of your company" being used for a reception.

   Invitations to a Roman Catholic wedding may replace the phrase "at the wedding (marriage) of..." with "at the marriage in Christ of...." They may also add, beneath the groom's name, "and your participation in the offering of the Nuptial Mass."

11. An invitation to a ceremony alone usually does not include a request for a reply but you may request a reply to a ceremony and/or reception invitation by including "R.s.v.p.," "Please respond," "Kindly respond," or "The favour of a reply is requested." You may also request a response date if it is necessary for

seating arrangements or the caterer. If the address to which the reply is to be sent is different from that which appears in the invitation itself, you may use "Kindly send reply to" followed by the correct address.

12. "Honour" and "favour" are always spelled with a "u," the more formal British variation.

13. Traditionally, your surname is not listed on the invitation, unless it is different from that of your parents, unless you and the groom are hosting the wedding yourselves, unless you have a professional title, or unless you have been married before. As a contemporary bride, however, it is acceptable to list it under any circumstances.

14. Titles such as "Mr.," "Miss," "Ms.," and "Dr." should be consistent for the bride and groom; use or omit them both. It has become quite common, however, to see only the bride's first and middle name, if she has one, with the groom's name listed in full, "Sarah Vanessa" and "Mr. William David Macfarlane." The same rule applies to the use of middle names–either use them for both or omit them entirely.

15. If your father, the groom, or the groom's father (when his name appears on the invitation) is a clergyman, physician, high elected official, or a member of the armed forces on active duty, you may use his professional title. When you, your mother, or the groom's mother hold one of the above

positions or titles, it should also be included. Traditionally, the female's titles were dropped but that practice is almost never adhered to today. Titles can be abbreviated but are more properly written in full.

As a contemporary bride, you may be faced with countless situations that require a variation on the traditional, formal wording of invitations. Here are some examples and general guidelines.

Traditional Wording

Bride's parents are hosts–

Mr. and Mrs. Henry Harland Packham
request the honour of your presence
at the wedding of their daughter
Miss Jo Packham
to
Mr. Michael Frazier Rozzelle
Saturday, the twenty-sixth day of May
Nineteen hundred and ninety-three
at half after six o'clock
The Homestead
Eden, Utah

Bride's and groom's parents are hosts–

Mr. and Mrs. Malcolm Swenson
request the honour of your presence
at the marriage of their daughter
Miss Dee-Ann Swenson
to
Mr. Daniel Richard Hartman
son of
Mr. and Mrs. Richard Henry Hartman
Friday, the fourteenth of May
at six o'clock in the evening
Nineteen hundred and ninety-three
The Oakwood
Portland, Oregon

Special Circumstances

Bride and groom are hosts–

Miss Heidi Glassman
and
Mr. Douglas Kemp
request the honour of your presence
at their marriage
Saturday, the fifth of December
at seven o'clock in the evening
Nineteen hundred and ninety-three
Lake Shore Country Club
Laguna Beach

Bride is a professional; her parents are hosts–

Mr. and Mrs. Joseph James Hathaway
request the honour of your presence
at the marriage of their daughter
Dr. Mary Louise Hathaway
to
Mr. Grant Theodore Holden
Saturday, the twenty-first day of January
at seven o'clock in the evening
Nineteen hundred and ninety-three
Club Freemont
Smithfield, Illinois

Bride previously married; her parents are hosts–

Mr. and Mrs. Stephen John Thompson
request the honour of your presence
at the marriage of their daughter
Ms. Sarah Thompson Glazier
to
Mr. Allan David Shaw
Friday, the first of August
at seven o'clock in the evening
Nineteen hundred and ninety-three
The Hermitage
Providence, Rhode Island

Groom's parents are hosts–

Mr. and Mrs. Hal Wilcox
request the honour of your presence
at the marriage of
Miss Tina Annette Brady
to their son
Mr. Steven James Wilcox
Friday, the twenty-first day of June
at five o'clock in the evening
Nineteen hundred and ninety-three
Quincy House
Island Park, Montana

DIVORCED PARENTS

When your parents are divorced, the wedding invitation is usually issued by the parent who raised you. If neither parent is remarried, your mother's name always comes first. You may choose to leave off all titles such as "Mr." and "Mrs." when your parents are divorced. There are, however, several different sets of circumstances and combinations when it comes to divorced parents and stepparents. Some examples for these special situations follow:

Bride's parents are hosts; divorced and not remarried–

Mrs. Margaret Ann Howard
and
Mr. Steven Clay Howard
request the honour of your presence
at the marriage of their daughter
Miss Melissa Christine Howard
to
Mr. Robert Scott Shields
Wednesday, the fourteenth day of February
at five o'clock in the evening
Nineteen hundred and ninety-three
Cambridge Country Club
Savannah, Georgia

Bride's parents are hosts; divorced and remarried–

If both parents are remarried and both are contributing to the finances and hosting the festivities, then your mother's name comes first.

If only your father is contributing but both are acting as official hosts, then his name may come first.

If you are close to both sets of parents and stepparents, the invitation might read "at the marriage of their daughter."

Mr. and Mrs. Edward Carl Black
and
Mr. and Mrs. Craig Jerome Bingham
request the honour of your presence
at the marriage of
Miss Celeste Ann Bingham
to
Mr. William Brian Huston
Monday, the eighteenth of March
at seven o'clock in the evening
Nineteen hundred and ninety-three
Hillsborough Lodge
Manchester, New Hampshire

Bride's mother and stepfather are hosts–

Mr. and Mrs. Robert William Smith
request the honour of your presence
at the marriage of Mrs. Smith's daughter
Miss Cortney Virginia Miller
to
Mr. John David Bass
Friday, the fifteenth of November
at six o'clock in the evening
Nineteen hundred and ninety-three
Jamesport Inn
St. Louis, Missouri

Bride's father and stepmother are hosts–

Mr. and Mrs. Thomas Jeffery Jones
request the honour of your presence
at the marriage of Mr. Jones' daughter
Miss Tracy Jennifer Jones
to
Mr. Richard Carlos Marti
Saturday, the eleventh day of July
at four o'clock in the evening
Nineteen hundred and ninety-three
Princeton Place
Oak Park, Illinois

Groom's parents are hosts; divorced and not remarried–

Mrs. Blanche Louise Checketts
and
Mr. James Jay Checketts
request the honour of your presence
at the marriage of
Miss Carole Meloney Chapman
to their son
Mr. Thomas James Checketts
Friday, the sixth of September
at seven o'clock in the evening
Nineteen hundred and ninety-three
Our Lady of the Madeline Cathedral
Durham, North Carolina

One divorced parent sponsoring the wedding with someone else such as a close relative or a live-in partner–

Mrs. Sylvia Jane Bergman
and
Mr. Henry John Martin
request the honour of your presence
at the marriage of Mrs. Bergman's daughter
Miss Carolyn Diane
to
Mr. Charles Edward Stanford
Saturday, the fourth day of August
at seven o'clock in the evening
Nineteen hundred and ninety-three
First Presbyterian Church
Ventura, California

DECEASED PARENT(S)
One living parent hosts–

Mrs. Blaine D. Edwards
requests the honour of your presence
at the marriage of her daughter
Miss Tiffany Lynn Edwards
to
Mr. Mark Douglas Bennington
Monday, the eighteenth of May
at seven o'clock in the evening
Nineteen hundred and ninety-three
Hampton Inn
Morristown, Pennsylvania

A deceased parent can be mentioned in the wedding announcement in the newspaper but is not usually included on the invitation for two reasons: First, an invitation is issued to share an occasion together; and, second, a wedding is a happy time and this might strike a note of sadness for some family members and guests. If, however, it is very important to you to include the deceased parent's name, you need to make certain that it does not appear that the invitation is issued by the deceased. It can be written as follows:

Together with their families
Janice Lynn Foley
daughter of Lisa Foley and the late John Craig Foley
and
Marcus Gregory Arnold
son of Mr. and Mrs. James Henry Arnold
request the honour of your presence
at their marriage
Friday, the fifth of August
Nineteen hundred and ninety-three
Heritage Manor
Baltimore, Maryland

Someone other than a parent hosts–

In this case, the relationship may or may not be mentioned in the invitation.

Mr. and Mrs. Keith David Hodson
request the honour of your presence
at the marriage of their niece
Miss Judi Lynn Rusk
and
Mr. Theodore Martin Peterson
Saturday, the twenty-sixth day of May
Nineteen hundred and ninety-three
at half after six o'clock
St. Peter's Cathedral
Des Moines, Iowa

If you are older and are getting remarried and if the married children of you and the groom are hosting the wedding, the children should be listed in alphabetical order.

Mr. and Mrs. Michael William Bingham
Mr. and Mrs. James Andrew Freemont
Mr. and Mrs. Daniel Spencer Wood
request the honour of your presence
at the marriage of their parents
Ms. Mary Hawkins Wood
and
Mr. David Andrew Freemont
Friday, the fifteenth of November
at six o'clock in the evening
Nineteen hundred and ninety-three
First Baptist Church
Greenville, South Carolina

Double ceremony–

While following the traditional wording, a few new rules apply here. If one bride is older, her parents and her name are mentioned first in the invitation. If both brides are the same age, the parents' names and brides' names are alphabetized. If the brides are sisters, the older one is named first.

Mr. and Mrs. Daniel Lee Chapman
request the honour of your presence
at the marriage of their daughter
Miss Leigh Ann Chapman
to
Mr. James Louis Dunham
and
Mr. and Mrs. Frederick Matthew Schultz
request the honour of your presence
at the marriage of their daughter
Miss Catherine Jane Schultz
to
Mr. Samuel Thomas Johnson
Saturday, the eighteenth day of June
at seven o'clock in the evening
Nineteen hundred and ninety-three
San Diego Yacht Club
San Diego, California

Guidelines for emphasizing the religious aspect of the ceremony–

Catholic

Mr. and Mrs. Raymond Lyle Swenson
request the honour of your presence
at the Nuptial Mass
at which their daughter
Sidney Jane
and
Mr. Robert Allen Michell
will be united in the
Sacrament of Holy Matrimony
Saturday, the ninth of April
at four o'clock in the evening
St. Ann's Cathedral
Auburn, New York

A special enclosure card may be sent to a small number of close friends and relatives that says:

You are cordially invited
to join the wedding party
in receiving Holy Communion
at this Nuptial Mass

Jewish

The phrasing on Jewish wedding invitations will vary depending on whether the ceremony is Orthodox, Conservative, or Reform. Check with your temple officiant.

Protestant

Mr. and Mrs. Ronald Steven Towers
are pleased to invite you
to join in a Christian celebration
of the marriage of their daughter
Jessica Gwen
to
Mr. Kirk Jay Kimble
Friday, the ninth of September
at five o'clock in the evening
First Presbyterian Church
1300 Lakeview Heights
Albuquerque, New Mexico

Reaffirming your wedding vows–

The honour of your presence
is requested at the reaffirmation
of the wedding vows of
Mr. and Mrs. Ellen Anne and Harold Thomas Matheson
Friday, the twentieth day of January
at seven o'clock in the evening
The Buckhead
8749 Lakeshore Drive

Wedding anniversary invitations–

October 2, 1943 – October 2, 1993
Mr. and Mrs. Jon Trent Hanson
request the pleasure of your company
at a dinner to celebrate
the Fiftieth Anniversary of their marriage
on Friday, the second of October
at seven o'clock
1444 South Oak Crest Drive

The favour of a reply
is requested.

Military titles–

You, the groom, or any of your parents may
use your military title, if desired. An officer
whose rank is equal to or higher than captain in
the army or lieutenant in the navy places the
title before his or her name. Those of lower
ranks may or may not place their rank on the
line below with the branch of service. Reserve
officers do not use military titles unless they are
on active duty. High-ranking officers of the
regular armed forces continue to use their titles
followed by their branch of service even after
retirement with "Retired" following their branch
of service.

General Evan J. Facer
United States Air Force

Bryan J. Folcom
Corporal, Signal Corps, United States Army

General James W. Macfarlane
United States Air Force, Retired

Contemporary

Contemporary wording is usually less formal and can be whatever you feel is appropriate for the formality and circumstances of the ceremony. Be certain to make your contemporary invitation warm but not too "gushy," concise rather than rambling, and in keeping with the mood of the celebration. You may want to be less formal and not write out times and dates. You will also need to remember to always include the following information:

1. Host's name
2. Bride's name
3. Groom's name
4. Ceremony site and address (if necessary)
5. Date
6. Time
7. Reception site (if necessary and an enclosure card is not included) and address (if necessary)

Examples for contemporary wording are–

Mr. and Mrs. Jerome Curtis Stanton
would like to invite you
to the marriage of their daughter
Elizabeth
and
Mr. William James Elliott
in their celebration of love
Friday, the twentieth day of January
at seven o'clock in the evening
The Buckhead
8749 Lakeshore Road

or

Mr. and Mrs. Fredrick John Martin
and
Mr. and Mrs. Anthony Paul Ritchins
invite you to share in
the marriage of their children
Kimberly
and
Jacob
Saturday, the eighteenth day of June
at seven o'clock in the evening
Nineteen hundred and ninety-three
San Diego Yacht Club
San Diego, California

Other appropriate phrases are–

invite you to share the joy
of the beginning of their new life together
as they exchange marriage vows

Our joy will be more complete
if you will share in the marriage of our daughter

We invite you to worship with us,
witness their vows and join us
for a reception following the ceremony

This celebration of love will be held on

Thoughts are often added, such as–

If you are unable to attend, we ask your presence in
thought and in prayer

A life of sharing, caring
a love of endless giving together

In the spirit of Christian joy
Carol Humphries
and
DeLoy Hughes Jensen
will vow their love to one another forever

Their families invite you to join them
in asking God's blessing upon this holy union

Special Considerations

If all of the guests are to be invited to both the ceremony and the reception that follows, a combined invitation may be sent without separate enclosure cards.

Mr. and Mrs. Henry Lawrence Scott
request the honour of your presence
at the marriage of their daughter
Victoria

to

Mr. Torrence Spencer
Thursday, the third day of July
at five o'clock in the evening
Saint Mary's Catholic Church
Sun Valley, Idaho
and afterward at
Sun Valley Golf and Country Club

R.s.v.p.
204 Antelope Way
Sun Valley, Idaho 68523

When one set of parents lives in a place a considerable distance from the ceremony site and they wish to have their friends meet you or the groom, either before or after the wedding, a reception may be planned and wording may be formal or informal. For example:

Formal wording (before the wedding)–

Mr. and Mrs. Ralph John Balken
request the pleasure of your company
at a reception in honour of
Miss Jennifer Ann Pugmire
and
Mr. James William Balken
Tuesday, the first of August
at nine o'clock in the evening
Charter Square
16 Hans Boulevard

When friends meet hearts warm.

Proverb

**Informal wording on a folded invitation
(after the wedding)–**

On the outside, the names of the party hosts
are printed; on the inside, it may read:

You are cordially invited
to a cocktail reception
in honour of
Jennifer and James Balken
Friday, the sixteenth day of June
at five o'clock in the evening
The Ellington Estate
9384 Post Office Place

If you are planning a small wedding with a
limited number of friends, handwritten
invitations are sometimes more appropriate
than engraved or printed ones.

Even though there are no strict codes for
handwritten invitations, they are written by the
person hosting the wedding and read basically
the same as any informal invitation. They
should be written with blue-black or black ink
on very high quality paper. You might elect to
send them on fold-over cards with or without
printed or engraved names on the front fold.
They may read as follows:

Allison Bongoeben and Scott Jensen are being
married at St. John's Cathedral on Friday, the third
day of November, at four o'clock. We hope you
will be able to come to the ceremony, and
afterward to the reception.

Most sincerely,
(Signature of person hosting the wedding)

Invitation Worksheet

(Use this space to practice what wording is appropriate for your invitations.)

Invitation will read:

_____

_____

_____

_____

_____

_____

_____

_____

_____

_____

_____

_____

_____

_____

_____

_____

_____

_____

_____ Inserts or Enclosures

Besides the invitations, several cards may be placed in the inner envelope (or outer envelope, if you omit the inner one). They all face the flap, and all are placed in front of the invitation itself—facing the person inserting them—or, if it is a folded invitation, within the fold. They are printed on the same quality paper and in the same style as the invitation itself.

Possible insertions you may want to consider are as follows:

Ceremony Cards

If the guest list for the reception is larger than the list for the ceremony (due to size restrictions of the ceremony site, religious restrictions, or your preference for a small, intimate ceremony), then a specially worded invitation inviting all guests to the reception is sent with a special insertion card for the ceremony.

The invitation to the reception may read as follows–

Mr. and Mrs. Daniel David Durbano
request the pleasure of your company
at a wedding reception held in the honour of
Michelle Anne Durbano
and
Jeremy Kyle Winters
Friday, the third day of November
at four o'clock in the afternoon
Donovan Mansion
Trenton, New Jersey

The ceremony enclosure card may read–

Mr. and Mrs. Daniel David Durbano
request the honour of your presence
at the ceremony
at three o'clock in the afternoon
St. John's Cathedral

*Happiness seems made
to be shared.*

Jean Racine

Reception Cards

If the guest list for the church is larger than that for the reception, a separate card is enclosed with the wedding invitation for those who are to be invited to the reception (or small gathering which usually includes a sit-down meal).

You may also include a reception card if the reception is being held at a different site than the ceremony. This card is usually about half the size and identical in typeface, paper, and printing style as the invitation itself. "Breakfast" is used if the event takes place before 1 p.m. and "Reception" is used if the event takes place after 1 p.m.

Reception
immediately following the ceremony
Mission Bay Yacht Club

The favour of a reply is requested
9348 Steeplechase Drive
San Diego, California

or

Breakfast celebration
to follow ceremony
White Horse Lodge
3429 Quail Hollow Trail
Crystal Springs, Vermont

Pew Cards

If the ceremony is a large, formal affair, you may elect to enclose in the invitation small cards with "Pew Number ___ Bride's/Groom's Section" engraved on them. These are sent to those family members and close friends who have been selected to be seated in the reserved pews. These cards are to be taken with them to the ceremony and shown to the ushers escorting them to their seats.

Similar cards are sometimes engraved with "Within the ribbon," meaning that a certain number of pews are reserved for special guests but no specific pew is assigned. This phrase may appear on the lower left-hand corner instead of the special pew number. However, this general reservation format is used only for very large, very formal weddings.

Pew cards can be sent separately after the R.s.v.p.s have been returned so that you will know how many reserved pews will be needed and can assign the correct number of seats. They can be a postcard-type mailer sent separately but must be large enough to fit postal requirements or they can be placed inside the appropriate-sized mailing envelope.

They may read–

Please present this card
Saint Christopher's Catholic Church
Saturday, the fifteenth of March

Bride's Reserved Section
Pew Number 1

If engraved cards are not being used, your
mother and the groom's mother may send their
own personal visiting cards for their own sides
of the church; or your mother may send her card
for both sides. They may have your mother's
name printed on the front side with, in her
handwriting, "Bride's Reserved Section" and the
pew number on the back side.

Admission/Ceremony Cards

Admission cards are only necessary when a
large, formal wedding is being held in a public
place such as a museum, historic site, cathedral
or church that attracts sightseers. To ensure
privacy under these circumstances, each guest is
asked to present his or her card to the usher at
the entrance. It is engraved in the same style as
the invitation and could read:

Please present this card
at
St. Vincent's Cathedral
Saturday, the seventh day of May

Rain Cards

These cards are enclosed when guests are invited to a garden wedding, informing them of an alternate location in case of inclement weather.

In case of rain
the wedding and reception
will be held at the
Biltmore Hotel
93429 Wilshire
at seven o'clock in the evening

Travel Cards

Travel cards are often used for very large, formal weddings to inform guests about wedding-day transportation arrangements, such as a designated bus to take them from their hotel, to the ceremony, and then to the reception. This card may also indicate parking locations and if fees or gratuities have been paid.

A special bus will leave
the Thomas Hotel
at two o'clock in the afternoon
and arrive back in Boston
at nine o'clock in the evening
Please present this card to the driver.

Parking provided
Cenessy Court
Lexington
Gratuities included
Please present this card to the parking attendant.

Maps

In today's mobile society and with so many wedding festivities including out-of-town guests, maps to the ceremony and/or reception are becoming frequent inserts in wedding invitations. They need to be drawn and printed in the same style as the invitation and are usually on a small, heavier card. If they are not printed in the same style as the invitations, they should be mailed separately. They should include topographical drawings as well as written directions, keeping in mind that guests may be coming from varying directions. Always have extras available at the ceremony site if the reception is in a different location for guests who may have forgotten theirs.

Long Weekend Wedding Cards

These cards are usually sent with invitations when the wedding festivities are being held in a resort area. They inform guests of the extended schedule, usually from Friday evening to Sunday afternoon, and about the additional events planned. This insert gives a schedule of events, suggestions for lodging and transportation, and sometimes an idea for appropriate attire for the different festivities.

At-Home Cards

If you and the groom wish your family and friends to know your new address, you may elect to insert an At-Home card.

Putting your married name on the card is optional but is often a good idea. It will help those recipients who file these cards in their address books not to forget *who* will be at home after May twenty- sixth! When included in a formal invitation, it may appear without a name. More often, at-home cards are sent with announcements and read as such:

Mr. and Mrs. Charles Gordon McComb
will be at home
after May twenty-sixth
1784 Twenty-seventh Street
Brigham City, Utah 84070

This can also provide the opportunity to inform family and friends if you plan to keep your maiden name.

Linda Carlson and Michael Tribe
will be at home
after June twelfth
1912 Harrop Street
Salt Lake City, Utah 84010

Response Cards

It should be universally understood that guests who receive an invitation to any wedding ceremony or reception should automatically and immediately respond as to whether or not they will be attending. This, however, does not always happen. You, therefore, may feel it necessary to include the R.s.v.p. right on the bottom left-hand corner of the invitation or you may elect to enclose response cards. These cards, traditionally, are not used for formal weddings where a personal reply is preferred and expected. They are used only when it is necessary to have an exact estimate for the caterer or if special seating arrangements need to be made.

When response cards are included, they need to be handled as tastefully as possible. Response cards, which are the smallest cards accepted by the postal service, should be at least 3 X 5 inches and should be engraved in the same style as the invitation. Addressed, stamped envelopes should be included as well.

Response cards may contain an R.s.v.p. date, with the remainder of the card being blank, allowing the guest to write a personal note:

The favour of your reply is requested
by Tuesday, the sixth day of September
M_____

Or they may read–

M_____

_____accepts

_____ regrets

Sunday, February fourteenth

The Parker Meridian Hotel

It is usually inappropriate to include "number of persons." Those whose names appear on the outer and inner envelopes are the only ones invited. If other members of the family do not have their names on the envelope, they should not be included. If you are having a formal wedding and you are using response cards, each couple, each single person, and all children should receive their own invitation.

Who can enjoy alone?

John Milton

Proofreading

Make certain that you and your stationer and a third party proofread all of the wording on all of your wedding stationery. This third person should probably be someone who is not closely connected to the wedding. You need someone uninvolved to question what those who are too close might miss!

The stationer should present you with a sample of your invitation several weeks before they are completed and delivered.

You will want to read the sample carefully and then compare it to the one you wrote out on the Invitation Worksheet on page 56.

The checklist below may help you when proofreading:

❑ **1.** Are the card size, color, weight, texture, type style, and designs correct?

❑ **2.** Are all of the names spelled correctly?

❑ **3.** Are all titles and middle names (or initials) used in a consistent fashion?

❑ **4.** Are the times and dates correct?

❑ **5.** Are the address and directions correct?

❑ **6.** Do the day of the week and the date correspond?

❑ 7. Are the words "honour," "favour," and "o'clock" spelled correctly?

❑ 8. Are all of the numbers spelled out?

❑ 9. Is the wording exactly as you requested it?

❑ 10. Do all of the lines begin and end at the appropriate space?

❑ 11. Are there periods after abbreviations?

❑ 12. Are commas and apostrophes in the right places?

Addressing and Stuffing Envelopes

The correct protocol for addressing and stuffing envelopes is as follows:

1. The outer and inner envelopes should be picked up before the invitations and inserts so that addressing can be completed beforehand.

2. You, your mother, and your honor attendant may address the invitations. Make certain you select helpers whose writing is the most pleasing and most legible. Always make certain the same person addresses the outer and inner envelopes for the same invitation.

3. All invitations are addressed by hand. Blue-black or black ink is always used. Typed or computer-generated addresses are only acceptable when special calligraphy-style fonts are being utilized.

4. On the outside envelope, all invited guests' names are written out in full, including the full middle name if it is known; if not, a middle initial may be used. Abbreviations are not permitted except for "Mrs.," "Mr.," and "Lt." when combined with "Colonel," "General," or "Commander." Titles such as "Doctor" should be written out in full.

5. Do not use "and Family." If the family includes small children and they are to be invited, their names are written under the names of their parents on the *inner* envelope only.

If there are two grown children, they may receive one invitation. The outer envelope reads:

Misses Nancy and Elizabeth Stark
9510 Camelback
Scottsdale, Arizona 12978

The inner envelope may read–

The Misses Stark and Guests

or

Nancy, Elizabeth and Guests

If the children are sons, the envelope is substituted with "Messrs."

If there is a combination of women and men, titles should be separate:

Miss Elizabeth Stark and Mr. John Stark
2029 Edgewood Cove
Aspen, Colorado 55893

6. If the smaller children are to be sent their own invitations, name the girls first on both envelopes. The outer envelope might read:

The Misses Makin
The Messrs. Makin
984 Arapean Way
Redmond, Washington 83472

The inner envelope then reads–

Judy, Mary, Andrew, and James

7. If the invited family has children over 18 living with their parents, they should receive their own invitation. If they are to invite guests, "and Guest" should be written on the inner envelope. The outer envelope reads:

Miss Nancy Louise Stark
9342 Sandpiper Lane
Kitty Hawk, North Carolina 77934

The inner envelope reads–

Miss Stark and Guest

or

Nancy and Guest

8. Adult men or women living at the same address each receive their own invitation.

9. Invitations are addressed to the husband and wife even if the sender knows only one member of the couple.

10. If the wife has a professional title, you may send one invitation with the wife's title and name on the line above the husband's. For example:

Dr. Anita Crane
Mr. David Crane
98 Center Street
Kingston, Ohio 59661

The inner envelope may read–

Dr. Crane and Mr. Crane

11. If a wife has retained her maiden name, the envelope is addressed:

Ms. Nancy Stacey
Mr. George Whitley
834 Panorama Drive
Whitefish, Montana 10053

The inner envelope may read–

Ms. Stacey and Mr. Whitley

or

Nancy and George

12. An unmarried couple living together may receive a joint invitation with their names listed alphabetically.

Ms. Josephine Riley
Mr. James Snider
934 Maple Street
Norfolk, Virginia 73948

The inner envelope reads–

Ms. Riley and Mr. Snider

13. When addressing invitations or announcements to members of the armed forces, it is appropriate to include their titles.

14. Women guests who are separated or divorced are often addressed with their given name and married surname: "Mrs. Lisa Jones"; if she is widowed, it is addressed "Mrs. George Jones."

15. Do not use symbols. For example, " Mr. & Mrs. Herbert John Pack" should be "Mr. and Mrs. Herbert John Pack."

16. The names of all streets, cities, states, and zip codes should be written out in full on the outside envelope.

17. A message is never handwritten on an engraved invitation.

18. Tissues that have been inserted in the invitations to keep the ink from smearing are left inside of the invitation.

19. On formal engraved invitations, the return address is usually embossed, without color, on the flap of the outside envelope of the wedding invitation.

20. All formal wedding invitations have two envelopes. The outer envelope is for the name and address of the person(s) to whom it is being sent. The inner envelope, which has no mucilage, contains the invitation, the tissue, and any enclosure cards. On the inner envelope is written the name of the person(s) to whom the invitation is being sent. The phrase "and Guest" is also added here as well as any children's names, which should be written on the second line under their parents' names. Nicknames may be used here if desired. No address is written on the inner envelope.

On the inside envelopes of invitations to relatives who are very dear to you or your intended, "Aunt Kate and Uncle George" or "Grandmother" may be written in your handwriting or the groom's. In either case, the same person must then address the envelope so the handwriting matches.

21. When the invitations have two envelopes, they are assembled as indicated below:
- **a.** The larger, formal invitation is folded in half across the middle.
- **b.** Any additional enclosures are placed inside of the invitation.
- **c.** The response card, with its lettering facing up, is placed under the flap of the response-card envelope. The response

card and its envelope are placed inside
of the invitation under any additional
enclosures (or on top, if it is the smallest)
with the lettering of the response card
facing up.

d. The invitation is held shut and a small
piece of tissue paper is placed over the
lettering on the invitation.

e. The invitation is placed inside of the
inner envelope with the front of the
invitation facing the back flap of the
envelope. The inner envelope is not
sealed.

f. The inner envelope is placed inside of the
outer envelope. The handwritten names
on the inner envelope should be facing
the back of the outer envelope. (Traditionally, this was inserted just the
opposite.)

g. Seal the outer envelope, making certain it
contains both the address of the person to
whom you are sending it and your return
address.

22. Have one invitation, complete with
enclosure cards, weighed by the postal service to
make certain of the exact amount of postage that
will be necessary.

23. Engraved or printed invitations should be
mailed four weeks before the ceremony.
Handwritten informal invitations should be
mailed two to three weeks before the ceremony.

24. Separate the local and out-of-town
invitations.

25. Stamp the outer envelope and mail. It is a nice idea to use commemorative stamps; the Post Office has an entire line of stamps available which are ideal for these types of mailings. Always send invitations first class, never by metered mail.

26. Mail all invitations at the same time. It is not advisable to bundle the invitations. Take the time to mail them from several different locations. There have been many horror stories of invitations being grouped, set aside, and never delivered.

Additional Printed Material

Printed Gift Receipt or Acknowledgment Cards

If you are very, very busy before the wedding, or have an extraordinarily large number of gifts, you can send preprinted cards that state you received the gift and that you will be sending a personal thank you later. *This does not ever replace a handwritten thank-you note;* it is a courtesy that informs the guests that their gift has arrived safely.

The card may say–

Miss Laurie Nord
has received your wedding gift and
will take pleasure in writing you
later of her appreciation.

Ceremony Programs

Ceremony programs add a personal touch to your wedding. If the wedding is formal, they should be printed to match the invitations and nicely bound. They make wonderful souvenirs for all who attend. They also are an unintrusive way to let guests know who is who, the soloist's name, and other useful information.

Programs are often especially helpful during some religious services where guests are to join in. If several of your guests are of another denomination, the program will act as a useful and much-appreciated guide.

The ushers can hand the programs to the guests as they are escorted to their seats or they can be placed at the front of the church in a decorative container. They include the following:

✦ The names of the participants.

✦ Information about the order and content of the ceremony.

✦ Lists of musical selections and readings.

✦ Biographies of participants.

✦ Thoughts on marriage or a short prayer.

Reception Favors
Place Cards

For larger, formal receptions that include a sit-down dinner, place cards are used to let guests know where they should be seated. They help the caterer know how many tables to set, they let the guests know how many people should be seated at each table, and they are a good way of putting people together so they feel comfortable and have the opportunity of meeting new friends and relatives.

The place cards are laid out on a table at the entrance to the reception. They are placed in alphabetical order for ease in locating. The tables are numbered so the guests can find the appropriate table.

Place cards come in a limited number of traditional designs and an unlimited variety of contemporary designs. The most traditional is the folded card but regardless of the design they all must contain the same information. The following is necessary information:

✦ Yours and the groom's names on the first line.

✦ The date on the second line.

✦ The third line is left blank so you may write in the guest's name.

✦ The fourth line is for the table number.

Printed Menus

For formal luncheons or dinners, individual souvenir menus of the meal may be placed on each person's plate at the table. These should be printed in the same style as the wedding invitation. They can be adorned with a decorative border, printed on the hotel stationery with the hotel's crest, or printed on something very unusual like a 9- inch "ribbon" of chintz or silk. The menu should contain the establishment's crest, your name, the groom's name, the menu, the wines, and—at the very bottom—the name of the city and the date.

Thank-You Scrolls

Thank-you scrolls are usually printed on some type of parchment paper and are rolled, tied with ribbon, and placed at each table setting at the reception. They usually have a short poem or sentiment thanking the guests for sharing the joy and celebration of you and the groom. They are not to be confused with thank-you notes, which are sent to each guest who gives a gift.

They may read–

As we begin our lives together
we extend our deepest thanks
for sharing with us a most joyous day
in celebration of our love.
Memories in years to come
will bring us so much pleasure.
Your thoughtfulness means more to us
than any words can measure.

Mike and Laurie
June 3, 1993

Napkins or Matchbooks

Napkins or matchbooks may also be ordered from your stationer. They usually have your and the groom's names, the wedding date, and sometimes a phrase or thought. They may also have a small graphic design printed above the names.

Party Favors

If, for a small reception or a special event like the rehearsal dinner, you wish to have party favors made, you may choose one of the following:

✦ Printed ornamental boxes filled with candy.

✦ Flowers, wrapped mints, or small sachet cushions wrapped with printed ribbons that have your names and the wedding date on them.

✦ Champagne glasses with your names and the wedding date printed or etched on them.

Too much of a good thing is simply wonderful!

Liberace

Wedding Announcements

Wedding announcements are primarily used if you have a very small wedding and/or reception. They are usually sent by your parents, or by you and the groom if you are older or this is a second marriage. Their purpose is to inform family and friends from out of town, those you have not seen for a while but still feel a kinship with, and all of the other people you would like to have invited to the wedding but were unable to.

✦ Announcements should never be sent to guests who were invited to the wedding and/or reception. One exception to this rule is if you had a very small ceremony and/or reception with handwritten invitations and you wish to send engraved announcements as a memento.

✦ Announcements are printed on the same paper and in the same style as the wedding invitations.

✦ They should be addressed before the day of the wedding and mailed the day of or the day following the ceremony.

✦ It is appropriate to insert an "At Home" card in the envelope with your announcement so recipients will know where to reach you.

✦ If a divorced couple remarries each other, no formal announcement is issued.

- Persons receiving an announcement are not obligated to send a gift; they will respond with a gift or acknowledgment as they desire.

One way of wording an announcement is as follows:

Mr. and Mrs. Charles Matthew MacCarthy
have the honour of announcing
the marriage of their daughter
Jennifer Ann
and
Nathan Daniel Buehler
on Saturday, the fifteenth of August
One thousand nine hundred and ninety-three
Jackson Hole, Wyoming

Announcements always include the day, month, and year on which the ceremony took place. (On formal invitations the year is optional.) They also always include the name of the city and state where the ceremony took place.

If a formal wedding is postponed or canceled after the invitations have been sent, all guests must be notified as soon as possible. When time permits, this is done with printed cards, rush-ordered from the stationer. They are to be the same style and formality as the original invitation. Notices are also sent to the newspapers immediately.

If time is short, invitations may be recalled by personal notes, telegrams, or telephone calls. Notes should be patterned after the invitations and signed by the person who issued the invitations. Calls should be made in the name of your parents. Reasons other than a death or illness in the family do not need to be mentioned.

The situations below may cause a postponement or cancellation of your wedding and should be handled as follows:

Emergency

If you or the groom becomes seriously ill or is seriously injured a day or two before the ceremony, invitations are recalled by family members via telephone or telegram.

Death in the Immediate Family

If a death occurs in the immediate family, it is up to you and the groom and the request of the dying party to decide whether or not the ceremony is to take place as planned or if the invitations are to be recalled by telephone and telegram. If time permits, a handwritten note may read:

Mr. and Mrs. Mark Edward Randall
regret that owing to a death in the family
the invitation to
their daughter's wedding
on Tuesday, the twenty-third of June
must be recalled

If the invitations are recalled, it is acceptable to have the ceremony as planned with only a few close friends and relatives in attendance.

Joy and sorrow are next-door neighbors.

Proverb

Engagement Broken After Invitations Have Been Mailed

If the engagement is broken after the invitations have been mailed and if there is adequate time before the day of the ceremony, engraved or printed notices are sent, recalling the wedding invitation. They may read as follows:

Mr. and Mrs. Stephen Paul Cunningham
announce that the marriage of their daughter
Elizabeth Lynn
to
Adam Jonathan Carter
will not take place

If the engagement is broken too close to the day of the wedding for printed notices, the invited guests are notified by telephone or telegram. No reason need be given for the broken engagement.

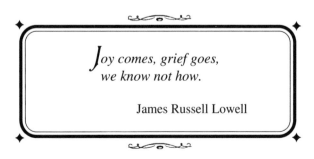

*Joy comes, grief goes,
we know not how.*

James Russell Lowell

Postponed Wedding

If for some reason the wedding has been postponed and another date has been set, guests may be notified by a new printed invitation (if there is time) in the same style as the original invitation. It may read as follows:

Mr. and Mrs. John Martin Faucett
announce that the marriage of their daughter
Heather Ann
to
Gordon Blake Cornell
has been postponed from
Thursday, the third day of January
until
Saturday, the seventeenth day of March
at seven o'clock in the evening
Eccles Community Art Center
2580 Jefferson Avenue
Ogden, Utah

If there is not sufficient time for a printed declaration, then the guests may be called by telephone or notified by telegram. No reason need be given for the postponement.

Thank-You Notes
or Cards

Thank-you stationery is available in both formal and informal styles. More formal styles are cards that are engraved or printed on the outside with your married name and your husband's name in a style that matches your invitations. Less formal styles can be printed with your name or have "Thank you" printed on the front.

It is inexcusable not to take the time to send each guest a thank-you note.

Basic points to remember when writing thank-you notes:

✦ Send a written thank-you note for every wedding gift you receive even if you have thanked the giver in person. Be certain to mention the gift in the body of the note and mention what you and/or the two of you plan to do with it. If you are uncertain about what the gift is or what to do with it, be vague and say something to this effect: "Thank you for the beautifully etched crystal piece. It will be given a place of honor in our new apartment."

✦ Send thank-you notes within two weeks of receiving a gift that arrives before the wedding, a month after the honeymoon for gifts received on your wedding day or shortly afterward. Write the date on the note, so if, through no fault of your own, the note is lost in the mail or misplaced upon arrival, the recipient will understand. (It is appropriate for guests to send gifts up to one year following the reception.)

+ If you are very, very busy before the wedding or have an extraordinarily large number of gifts, you can send preprinted acknowledgment cards that state you received the gift and that you will be sending a personal thank-you later. This does not ever replace a handwritten note; it is a courtesy that informs the guests that their gift has arrived safely.

+ Sign your notes with your maiden name before the wedding, your married name (if you plan to use it) after the wedding. Never send stationery with your married name on it before the wedding.

+ Encourage the groom to write his own thank-you notes, especially to his friends and relatives who gave gifts because of their association with him.

+ Customarily, the writer of the note signs it; the other name is mentioned in the body of the letter, for example: "Jon and I love the crystal vase...." Sign the note the way you and the groom feel most comfortable.

+ A thank-you note to a married couple may be addressed to the member of the couple you know the best with the spouse mentioned in the body of the note, or you may address it to them both.

+ It has become customary to write one thank-you note to a large group (such as co-workers) who send a joint wedding gift. It is this author's feeling, however, that individual thank-you notes are more thoughtful and gracious. No matter how much the investment was per person for the gift, each person should be thanked for his/her contribution and thoughtfulness individually. There are some instances, however, that group thank-you notes are never acceptable, even on a joint gift. For example, bridesmaids should always be thanked individually, as should relatives or friends who live away but contributed together to give you a nicer gift.

> *I would maintain that thanks are the highest form of thought, and that gratitude is happiness divided by wonder.*
>
> G. K. Chesterton

Eight Steps to the Perfect Thank-you Note

1. Address the envelope with the giver's name and address before you write the note.

2. Address the note to the person who gave the gift. Traditionally, you write to the woman if it is a married couple; contemporarily, however, you write to the person you know the best in the couple.

3. In the first sentence say thank you, mention the name of the person who is not addressed in the opening, and name the gift. For example, "Thank you so much for the crocheted afghan that you and Mr. Barker sent...." If you do not know what the gift is, simply describe it: "...the lovely monogrammed copper piece."

4. Mention something more about the gift, for instance, how much you have wanted one or how perfectly it fits into the decor of your new home. If the gift is money, tell them how you intend to use it. Mention your husband's name in this sentence: " Because Michael and I will both be attending school this fall, the alarm clock will be a big help in getting us to class on time."

5. Add one more thought. It may have something to do with the wedding, if the gift arrives before, or something to do with the honeymoon, if the notes are written upon your arrival home.

6. If it is prior to the wedding, sign off with a sincere salutation and your maiden name. Use your married name (if you choose to use it) after the wedding. Sign both first and last names only if you do not know the giver well.

7. Double-check to make certain that the correct thank-you note is in the correct envelope and check that name off of your list and be certain to record the date the note was written/sent. You may think you will remember which notes were written, but it can be very difficult. There is just too much happening, and the thank-you notes are too important to make a mistake on the names, to let time lapse too long before they are written and sent or to let them slip through the cracks altogether.

8. Stamp all of the envelopes at the same time and drop them in the mailbox yourself so you are certain the job is done correctly and in a timely manner.

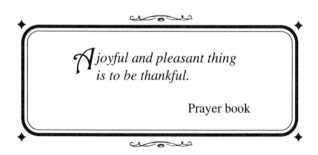

A joyful and pleasant thing is to be thankful.

Prayer book

*Let us celebrate this occassion
with wine and sweet words.*

Latin Proverb